ALL BERLIN
and Potsdam

Text, lay-out, design and printing by
EDITORIAL FISA ESCUDO DE ORO, S.A.

SCHIKKUS
VERLAG & GROSSHANDEL
GmbH & Co. KG
Otto-Suhr-Allee, 114 - 10585 BERLIN
Tel: (030) 364 077-0 - Fax: 3640 77 77

Photographs:
Lehnartz Berlin
Heinze von Hippel Berlin
Nuske Berlin
Rehberg Berlin
Schneider Berlin
Deutsche Luftbild
Stiftung
Preussische Schlösser und Gärten
Berlin-Brandenburg

ESCUDO DE ORO

CONTENTS

Paris Square and Brandenburg Gate.

Potsdam Square.

Berlin by night.

WELCOME TO BERLIN

Berlin is whole once more. This combative city, for so long divided, marginalised and, in spite of everything –on both sides of the wall– tenacious in its vision of a future, will now resume its growth as a reunified whole. Berlin is preparing for the day when it will once more be the great European metropolis it was in the past, and is taking on new activities, new perspectives and even a new physical appearance. Both the old and the new city are badly scarred, but these scars are worn with pride and awareness of what they signify. Berlin must not forget its history, but must hold it up as a reminder and an exhortation, as well as a touchstone for future development. In the same way that Berlin suffered the consequences of the Second World War and the subsequent division of Germany more than any other city, this new transformation, rebirth and resurgence, the future of this state, reunified here, in this marked city, is much more perceptible than anywhere else in the country.

On 9 November 1989, Berlin suddenly ceased to be an insular city, an outpost of the free world or a socialist showpiece, according to which side of the wall you were on, to become a revolving platform between the two worlds, the centre of the political, social, spiritual and cultural attention of a new world order, advancing at great speed. It happened here: on the night from 8 to 9 November 1989, the Berlin Wall, bulwark of socialism, suddenly became permeable. Like a fearful ghostly apparition, this symbol of disunity and

Perspective of the Spree river with the Cathedral and the Saint Nicholas district.

scorn for humanity had risen over the city on 13 August 1961, but the terrible cement spectre was finally dismantled and destroyed brick by brick by the people of the city. At the frontier posts and on the crown of the wall, strangers and friends alike embraced in tears of joy. Soon, drilling away like woodpeckers, the Berliners left the wall as full of holes as a Swiss cheese.

As suddenly as partition had plunged the nation into despair, relations between the formerly isolated western city and the hated GDR capital were restored. Berlin is now once more the capital of Germany and the seat of its government. Nowhere else has unity been achieved so clearly, so closely, as in this city, now restored again to its traditional place in history. Strange as it may seem, all this had humble beginnings, ironically enough in the guise of a divided city. Around the year 1200, two trading communities settled here, at the narrowest point of the Spree River Valley in Warschau-Berlin. These communities were Berlin and Cölln, separated by the Spree. The rival cities (Cölln is first mentioned in a document dating back to 1237, a date taken as a point of reference for determining the «birth» of Berlin) were united in 1307, when a joint government was formed. As a consequence of the colonisation of the regions to the east, this twin city enjoyed its first period of economic expansion, forming part of the Hanseatic League for 200 years.

After consolidation under the Hohenzollerns in 1442, this proud city became the residence of the Prince Electors, and the Hohenzollern dy-

General view of the Spree river.

nasty ruled over the destiny of the city for 500 years. In 1443, the castle in Cölln began to be built, though its final aspect, up to its destruction in 1950, owed more to the work of Andreas Schlüter in 1698.

Half the population of Berlin died during the Thirty Years' War (1618-1648), and only the wise policies of the «Great Elector», Friedrich Wilhelm, were able to give new impulse to the city once more, organising it as a severe, totalitarian state in the Prussian style. Under Friedrich Wilhelm, the city gave refuge to the persecuted French Huguenots and the Viennese Jews.

Later, immigrants from Bohemia, the Palatinate and elsewhere also found a welcome in Berlin, and all these people, converging on the city, brought new ideas, a more refined lifestyle and innovative craft techniques.

In 1701, the Great Elector's successor, his son, Friedrich III, was crowned in Königsberg as «First King of Prussia», and Berlin was made the capital and royal residence of the Kingdom of Prussia. His successor, Friedrich II, later venerated as «Old Fritz», continued the work begun by his father, turning Berlin into a great European city, not only in terms of

architecture but also from a spiritual point of view. The «Athens of the Spree», as the city was known due to its many classical-style buildings, was a city of the Enlightenment, as is attested to by the well-documented friendship between the king and the French philosopher Voltaire.

At the same time, Berlin continued to grow steadily, its population rising from 56,000 in 1720 to 147,000 in 1781. In this city of soldiers, one in four inhabitants belonged to the «military population», for Prussia was conceived, above all, as a «uniformed state».

In 1806, after the defeats at Jena

The Cathedral with the «Dom Aquaree».

and Auersted, Napoleon's victorious army entered the city through the Brandenburg Gate. The occupation lasted two years and in 1809 the court and government returned to the city from exile in Königsberg. Once more, the city enjoyed a new period of flowering in all areas of pre-industrial society. Wilhelm von Humboldt founded Friedrich Wilhelm University and the architect Karl Friedrich Schinkel and master landscape gardener Peter Joseph Lenné made a decisive contribution to the appearance of Berlin, which became, over the course of the 19th century,

the most important European industrial city. However, with the quashing of the civil uprisings of March 1848, all aspirations to a modern, liberal constitution were abandoned for the time being.

The second half of the 19th century was marked by the «Gründerjahre», or years of the German industrial revolution. Thanks to the close co-operation between capital, science and technology, numerous discoveries were made in Berlin, and modern factories, now internationally renowned, sprang up: Siemens (1847), Schering (1851), Agfa (1873) and AEG

(1883), to name just four of the best-known. When Bismarck achieved German unity in 1871, Berlin became the capital of the Reich and the residence of the Emperor. Tens of thousands emigrated to this new centre of empire, particularly from the eastern regions (which explains the saying «one out of two Berliners is from Breslau»). A period of great and lasting growth began, the city's population rising from 900,000 to 1.9 million inhabitants between 1871 and 1890. By 1910, the figure stood at 3.7 million. The Berlin transport system dates to the end of the 19th

View of Tauentzienstraße with the sculpture of «Berlin» and, in the background, the Emperor Wilhelm Commemorative Church.

Ruins of the Commemorative Church.

century, the first underground railway line having been opened in 1902. The magnificence and glory of the Wilhelm period lasted up until the year 1914.

At the end of the First World War, the monarchy was brought down in the wake of defeat. Kaiser Wilhelm I's exile in Holland marked the end of 500 years of Hohenzollern domination of Berlin. An ordinary citizen, Friedrich Ebert, was proclaimed president of the new republic. Through all this, Berlin continued to grow. The Great Berlin Law, passed in 1920, decreed the integration into the city of eight previously independent townships, 59 rural communities and 27 rural districts for form what became known as «Great Berlin», a huge metropolis divided into 20 administrative districts. At that time, the city had a population of 3.9 million. From the point of view of national politics, the «Roaring Twenties» were characterised by countless crises, strikes, demonstrations, inflation and unemployment. The desperate situation akin to a state of civil war, provided the opportunity for the national socialists to seize power. Berlin was the most important stage in the events even of the most shameful episode in German history, the Hitler dicta-

Brandenburg Gate.

Ruins of the Reichstag building, 1945.

INTRODUCTION

torship, from 1933 to 1945, for, as capital of the Reich, it became the centre of National Socialist party power. The city witnessed a period of repression, of popular identification with government policy, of the persecution and annihilation of the Jews and, finally, of its own spiritual and material destruction.

On 2 May 1945, Berlin, or what was left of it, surrendered. The city had become the most enormous ruin in Germany and the whole of Europe. Amongst the rubble, the women did all the work, keeping the wrecked city alive, as Berlin began to pick itself up once more. The victorious Allies agreed the partition of Germany,

and Berlin found itself split into four sectors. Shortly afterwards, what later became known as the Cold War began, converting Berlin into a frontier town, and the cause of much bitterness. After the monetary reform of the west, the Soviets blockaded the three western sections of the city and from 24 June 1948 to 12 May 1949, Berlin was supplied by cargo transported in an airlift by Rosinen-bomber planes. A few months after it was agreed to make a fresh start the city was politically divided into West Berlin, GDR capital, and Berlin part of the Federal Republic. From this moment on, East and West took different paths.

However, it seemed impossible to resume normal daily life. The popular uprising of 17 June 1953 was put down with the help of Soviet tanks. West Berlin became a springboard for escape for East Berliners and East Germans in general untilthe unthinkable happened: on 13 August 1961 a wall began to be built on the East German side which split the city of Berlin in half. This sinister symbol of German division, cutting through the capital for a length of 155 kilometres, was the cause of over 80 deaths and countless tears. Just a few fig

Part of the walls of the Bernauer street.

Wall in the Potsdam Square.

Views of the old Wall with graffiti.

Berlin has been a reunified city once more since 3 October 1990.

The Brandenburg Gate on the night of 3 October 1990: the people of Berlin celebrate the reunification of the city.

Brandenburg Gate.

ures to illustrate the terror behind this cruellest of constructions: 66.5 kilometres of barbed wire, 302 look-out towers, 20 bunkers, 105 trenches with anti-vehicle barriers, 127 contact and signals fences, 124 passages and 259 runs for guard-dogs. The West refused to give up Berlin, however, and on 26 June 1961, US President John Kennedy won the trust and admiration of the inhabitants of the city with his legendary declaration before all those gathered at the Schönberg town hall: «I am a Berliner». Tension was slightly eased as a result of the 1972 agreement reached by the four powers and the later «Fundamental Treaty» between the two Germanies. Nonetheless, anoth-

er 17 years of separation passed before the frontiers of the divided city could be opened up once more. In November 1989, after weeks of disturbances and demonstrations, the SED-run East German state was dismantled by its own people. The peaceful revolution, one of the few revolutions in history to have taken place without bloodshed, finally ended on November 9 with the opening of the wall. For days, the streets and squares of Berlin were packed with happy people who could hardly believe this radical turn-about in their own history. Thousands of people gathered at the Brandenburg Gate and began climbing the wall. Overjoyed, they toasted one anoth-

er and gave a warm welcome to al the «polis» as they entered the West Relations between East and West were hurriedly restored over the following days and, gradually, after a 29-yea reign, the wall began to fall.
Since Christmas 1989, both the people of Berlin and visitors to the city car once more cross the Brandenburg Gate in either direction, as they please What is taken for granted in the rest of the world is fully appreciated ir Berlin. Almost overnight, the former great metropolis, which had endured many years of mistreatment and paralysis, once again became the centre of attention of all the nations of the world. History is nowhere so tangible, so palpable as in Berlin.

Quadriga of the Brandenburg Gate.

THE BRANDENBURG GATE

The Brandenburg Gate and Paris Square.

German reunification took place on 3 October 1990 and on 20 June 1991 the German parliament, the Bundestag, decided to make Berlin the capital of the nation, a status the city has enjoyed since 1999.

THE BRANDENBURG GATE

After the peaceful revolution of November 1989 and the fall of the Berlin Wall, the Brandenburg Gate at last recovered its true function, and Berliners and visitors alike could freely pass from west to east and from east to west.

Over the «Gate of Peace», which is the name it was given when inaugurated in 1791, stands the majestic statue of the Goddess of Victory riding a chariot towards the old city centre, the work of Johann Gottfried Schadow.

The gate, built at the behest of King Frederick William II, renders homage to Frederick the Great as general and ruler. The architecture Carl Gotthard Langhans, commissioned to carry out the work, took his inspiration from the propylaeum on the Acropolis in Athens.

In 1807, Napoleon ceased the Victory sculpture as the spoils of war and it was not returned until 1814, when the French were defeated at Leipzig. Friedrich Wilhelm III then commissioned the addition of the cross and the Prussian eagle to the figure of Victory. The work was badly damaged towards the end of the Second World War, and was repaired in 1958. The gate was restored once more in 1991 on the occasion of the bicentenary of its construction.

The Brandenburg Gate marks the end of **17 June Street** and, with **Pariser Platz,** the beginning of the splendid **Unter den Linden («Under the Linden Trees») boulevard**, joining the western and eastern sections of the re-unified city.

16

Overall aerial view of the centre of Berlin (Berlin Mitte).

THE HISTORIC CENTRE OF BERLIN (BERLIN MITTE)

To the east, beyond the Brandenburg Gate and the Reichstag, lies the old city centre of Berlin. The aerial photograph on this page shows an overall view of Central Berlin (Berlin Mitte): behind the Brandenburg Gate, Paris Square (Pariser Platz) leads into the green avenue of Unter den Linden, stretching as far as the Cathedral, the Palace of the Republic and, a little further on, Alexanderplatz. This is where the **Television Tower** rises, its pointed spire pointing straight up at the Berlin sky. Built in 1969, its 365-metre height makes this the tallest building in the city. On sunny days, the «Pope's Revenge», a cross-shaped reflection certainly not intended to occur by the SED leadership, can be seen on its shining globe. The black building in front of the tower is the old East Berlin shopping centre.

Unter den Linden, one of the most sumptuous avenues in the city, reveals the glories of its Prussian past. Some of the interesting buildings between this avenue and the River Spree include the old Arsenal, the Unter den Linden National Opera House, the New Guardhouse, the seat of the Humboldt University and the equestrian statue of Frederick the Great.

The **Arsenal (Zeughaus)** was built between 1695 and 1706 by the architects A. Nering, M. Grünberg and A. Schlüter and is the most representative work in the Berlin baroque style. Originally built as an armoury for the young Prussian state, the building has housed the **Museum of German History (Deutsches Historisches Museum)** since 1952. Reminding visitors of its original purpose, the inner courtyard features an exhibition of the death-masks of 22 soldiers.

THE HISTORIC CENTRE OF BERLIN (BERLIN MITTE)

The old Arsenal, now the seat of the German History Museum.

The Palace of the Crown Prince.

The **Unter den Linden National Opera House (Staatsoper Unter den Linden)** dates from 1741-1743 and is the work of the architect and painter Knobelsdorff. However, after its destruction by fire in 1843, the opera house was rebuilt in classical style by Carl Gotthard Langhans.

The **New Guardhouse (Neue Wache)** was built for the Royal Guard between 1817 and 1818 by Karl Friedrich Schinkel. Inside is the monument in memory of the victims of fascism and militarism, a sculptured by Käthe Kollwith which takes its inspiration from the Pietà.

What is now the seat of the **Humboldt**

The New Guard.

Humboldt University.

View of Unter den Linden with the equestrian statue of Frederick the Great.

National Opera House and the St. Hedwig's Cathedral.

University was built between 1748 and 1753 as the residence of Prince Heinrich, younger brother of Frederick the Great. After Heinrich's death in 1809, the palace was converted into a university founded by the German politician and philologist Wilhelm von Humboldt.

The **equestrian statue of Frederick the Great** was erected in 1851 in memory of the king. The pedestal below features representations of different personalities of the time, including Leopold I, Prince of Anhalt-Dessau, the philosopher Immanuel Kant and the writer Gotthold Ephraim Lessing.

Behind the Unter den Linden National Opera House is **St. Hedwig's Cathedral**, immediately recognisable by the green reflections of its dome. The construction of this church in honour of the patron saint of Silesia was an attempt by Frederick the Great to appease the prince of Silesia following the military occupation of the region. It was built between 1747 and 1778 under the direction of the architect Knobelsdorff, who took as his model the Pantheon in Rome. In 1923, the church was elevated to the category of Basilica. Badly damaged during the Second World War, it was restored (1952-53), the interior now featuring modern decorative elements. Not far from the cathedral is what is for many the most beautiful square in Berlin: **Gendarmenmarkt** (Market of the Gendarmes), thus named after the barracks and stables installed here by the Gens d'Armes regiment of cuirassiers in the times of Friedrich Wilhelm I, though it is also known

View of the interior of the French Church, in Gendarmenmarkt.

View of Gendarmenmarkt with the Schinkel Theatre and the French Church.

THE HISTORIC CENTRE OF BERLIN (BERLIN MITTE)

as Academy Square. Presiding over one side of the square is the **Schinkel Theatre (Schinkelsche Schauspielhaus)**, masterpiece of the architect of the same name, built in 1818 after the old French Comedy Theatre, built in 1774, burnt down in 1817. Its last director was Gustaf Gründgens. Reduced to ruins in the Second World War, the theatre was rebuilt in 1967, and is now used as a concert hall. On the left is the **German Cathedral (Deutscher Dom)** and on the right is the **French Cathedral (Französischer Dom)**, both built between 1701 and 1708, though their imposing domes were not added until 80 years later by Carl von Gontard. The site was badly damaged during the war and in 1977 reconstruction began, a model for processes of the kind. Visitors can go up to the top of the tower of the

French Cathedral to enjoy fine views. The French Cathedral also houses the Huguenot Museum, devoted to the history of these refugees, whilst the German Cathedral has been the site since 1996 of a permanent exhibition entitled «Questions of History of Germany», forming an overview of German parliamentary history since 1800.

We now return to the National Opera, besides which is **Bebel Square**, formerly Opera Square. Here we find the **Old Palace (Alte Palais)**, whose main front gives onto Unter den Linden. The palace was built by Carl Ferdinand Langhans between 1834 and 1837 for Crown Prince Wilhelm. Nearby is the **Royal Library (Könichliche Bibliothek)**, known to the local people as the «commode» (Kommode) due to the unusual arched shape of its front. Unlike the classi-

cal buildings which surround it, the Royal Library is a construction with a marked baroque air. Rebuilt after the war, it now houses different institutions attached to nearby Humboldt University. On 10 May 1932, Opera Square was the scene of the gruesome burning of books, in which works without number, «the writings and books of immorality and demoralisation», including volumes by Thomas and Heinrich Mann, Kurt Tucholsky, Albert Einstein and Sigmund Freud, amongst many others, were fed to the flames.

At the end of Unter den Linden, beside the River Spree, is **Berlin Cathedral (Berliner Dom)** with its dome, as huge as it is beautiful, built in 1894 by Julius Raschdorff for Wilhelm II. Besides the great dome, the building also features such interesting elements as the Hohenzollern

The Royal Library.

Berlin Cathedral.

baptism chapel, the Kaiser's staircase and the tomb of the Elector and his wife Dorothea.

Behind the cathedral, on so-called **Museum Island (Museums-Insel)** are the classical museums of Berlin: the **Ancient Museum (Altes Museum)**, built in 1830 under the direction of the architect Schinkel, containing different art collections; the **National Gallery (Nationalgalerie)**, a neo-classical building constructed between 1866 and 1876; the **Pergamon Museum (Pergamonmuseum)**, another neo-classical building going back to the early-19th century, and which houses, amongst many other fine pieces, the Pergamon Altar, the gate to the market in Miletus, and the famed Istar Gate, which gave entrance to the ancient city of Babylon; and, finally, at the northernmost point of this «island», the **Bodemuseum**, named after the curator and art historian Wilhelm von Bode, and which also displays various art collections. Preceding all these museums is the **Lustgarten** (Leisure Garden), a spacious esplanade which originally formed part of the gardens of Berlin Castle, now lost and which served as the scene of military parades from the times of Friedrich Wilhelm I.

Opposite the cathedral, in Schloßplatz or Palace Square, once stood the

23

THE HISTORIC CENTRE OF BERLIN (BERLIN MITTE)

Aerial view of Museum Island, with the Cathedral.

Pergamon Museum: Pergamon Altar.

Pergamon Museum: gate to the market in Miletus.

THE HISTORIC CENTRE OF BERLIN (BERLIN MITTE)

The Ancient Museum from Lustgarten.

The National Gallery.

THE HISTORIC CENTRE OF BERLIN (BERLIN MITTE)

Image of the disappeared Imperial Palace.

The old Council of State of the GDR.

View of the River Spree with the Marstall (now the City Archive), the Palace of the Republic and Cathedral.

The River Spree and Bodemuseum.

THE HISTORIC CENTRE OF BERLIN (BERLIN MITTE)

View of Alexanderplatz with the Television Tower (built between 1965 and 1969).

Imperial Palace, its ruins finally demolished in 1950 to make way for the construction of the **Council of State (Staatsratsgebäude)** and the **Palace of the Republic (Palast der Republik).** The latter, a robust construction in steel and cement with a glazed front, completed in 1976, was where the East German People's Chamber met and where, in 1990, the first democratically-elected government of East Germany approved reunion with the Federal Republic. Behind this building, the former royal stables, built in 1670 by Michael Matthias Smids, now house the City Library and Archive **(Stadtbücherei und -archiv).**

Beyond Unter den Linden is **Alexanderplatz.** Since the construction of the Television Tower, this square no longer has the same appearance as in the times of the writer Alfred Döblin. In his most famous novel, Berlin Alexanderplatz (1929), Döblin describes in his vibrant style the vitality which once characterised this square. The Second World War reduced it to ruins, however, and the East German authorities subsequently made it the scene for military parades. Nonetheless, Alexanderplatz continues even today to be one of the nerve-centres of the city.

At one end of the square is, as we have said, the **Television Tower**, built in 1969 and 365 metres in height. The Telecafé, situated 200 metres up in the revolving viewpoint, offers complete panoramic views of the city and environs.

Beside the square is the **Red Town Hall (Rotes Rathaus),** whose name is due to the reddish stone in which it was built by Friedrich Waese between 1861 and 1869. After the events of 1989, round table sessions began to be held here. A terracotta frieze running around the outside of the building narrates the history of Berlin from its origins to the founding of the Reich in 1871, whilst in-

side are glass cabinets containing the coats of arms of the districts of the city. For its part, the **Old Town Hall (Altes Stadthaus)** is the former seat of the East German Council of Ministers.

Opposite the Red Town Hall is **St. Mary's Church (Marienkirche)**, mentioned in a document going back as far as the year 1274, though greatly altered over the course of the centuries. Between the church and the Town Hall is the **Fountain of Neptune**, designed in 1891 by Reinhold Begas. Also of interest in Alexanderplatz is the **World Clock (Weltzeituhr)**, which

The Old Town Hall.

THE HISTORIC CENTRE OF BERLIN (BERLIN MITTE)

The World Clock.

tells the exact time in no fewer than 27 places all over the globe.

Older than Unter den Linden Avenue, Alexanderplatz or even the Kurfürstendamm is the **Saint Nicholas district (Nikolaiviertel),** which lies south of Alexanderplatz beside the Spree, for this is the site of the first human settlement in Berlin. In the centre of the district is the **Church of St. Nicholas (Nikolaikirche)** with its two pointed towers, visible from all around. The original building date from the year 1230, but its present aspect owes more to the large-scale alterations carried out in the late-14th century, and the towers were not built unt

St. Mary's Church and Fountain of Neptune.

The River Spree and St. Nicholas district.

877. The houses clustering around he church, with restaurants and other elegant establishments, form a high-v attractive setting. The church and istrict were almost completely de-troyed during the Second World Var and reconstruction did not begin ntil 1982. Around what was once ne Milk Market stand buildings with nostalgic, historic air whose orig-inal sites were in the district itself or elsewhere. Such is the case, for ex-ample of the «**Zum Nussbaum**» (Walnut) inn, which formerly stood on the Island of the Fishermen.

Another interesting building in the Saint Nicholas district is the **Ephraim Palace (Ephraimpalais)**, on the corner of Mühlendamm and Poststraße. Built in 1764 in rococo style, the palace bears witness even now to the wealth of the former owner of the rights to coin money in Berlin. But counterfeit money existed even in those days, and the banker Veitel Ephraim spent many years in prison for producing coins with a fine gold coating rather than of solid gold. This elegant palace now forms part of the Berlin City Museum (Stadtmuseum

THE HISTORIC CENTRE OF BERLIN (BERLIN MITTE)

The Church of St Nicholas...

...in St. Nicholas district.

The Church of St Nicholas.

Jungfern Bridge.

Sumptuous row of balconies of Ephraim's Palace.

Artistic fountain in the Saint Nicholas district.

Statue of St George and the Dragon.

THE HISTORIC CENTRE OF BERLIN (BERLIN MITTE)

«Friedrichstadtpalast».

Popular theatre (Volksbühne).

Tacheles (house of art).

Monbijou Park.

«Strandbad-Mitte» ("bathing beach" in Berlin Mitte).

Theaterplatz: Chamber Room and German Theatre.

Berlin) and is used as the venue for exhibitions on different themes relating to the city.

Both the church and the district bear the name of Saint Nicholas, patron saint of sea traders. The restored houses lining the right bank of the Spree allow us to imagine the trade and traffic in what used to be the twin city of Berlin-Cölln. To stroll around old Berlin is to go on a journey into the past. The sculpture of a fountain represents Saint George fighting the dragon. On another fountain we see the bear of Berlin holding the city coat of arms in his powerful claws. A publicity pillar informs us of the cultural activities of the moment. The craftsmen's guild signs tell us the trade plied by the inhabitants of the different buildings before we draw near. The Saint Nicholas district is a veritable journey through Berlin's rich history and as such is a visit not to be missed.

Before leaving the historic city centre, we should point out one or two final points of interest here. The first is Theaterplatz (Theatre Square), in the north of Berlin Mitte. Here we find the **German Theatre (Deutsches Theater)** and the **Chamber Room (Kammerspiele)**, two old venues which are still amongst the most important in Berlin. The first is devoted, above all, to productions of classical works, whilst the programme of the second leans more towards the comedy. Finally, a visit is recommended to the **Flohmarkt, or Flea Market**, in Arkonaplatz (also in the northern part of Mitte), where antique objects are bought and sold each Saturday and Sunday, from 10.00 to 16.00.

THE HISTORIC CENTRE OF BERLIN (BERLIN MITTE)

Unter den Linden Avenue, Friedrichstrasse station and the IHZ (International Commerce Centre).

View from the Friedrichstrasse towards Unter den Linden.

Friedrichstrasse Station.

The Kreuzberg Waterfall, at the top of which stands the Monument to Kreuzberg, erected in 1821 to commemorate of the war of liberation against Napoleon.

KREUZBERG

North of Tempelhof Airport in Victoriapark in the Kreuzberg district is one of the few elevated sites in the city. This is where, in 1894, the municipal director of gardens, Hermann Mächtig, drew up plans for the **Kreuzberg waterfall** as we see it today, taking as his model a waterfall in the Riesengebirge Mountains. From an impressive height of 66 metres, the water tumbles noisily down, descending terrace after terrace to reach Grossbeerenstraße to vanish without trace under the asphalt of the great city. At the top of the falls, at the point where the water issues forth, rises the **Monument to Kreuzberg (Kreuzbergdenkmal)**, a 66-metre high iron tower erected in remembrance of the 1813-1815 wars of liberation against the forces of Napoleon. The work of Karl Friedrich Schinkel, the monument was inaugurated in 1821. This elevated spot also commands fine views over the city.

Further north, in Askanischer Square, stands the entrance to what was once the most important long-distance railway station in Berlin and the third-largest in Europe: **Anhalter Station (Anhalter Bahnhof)**. Trains south to Leipzig, Dresden, Vienna, Rome or Athens used once to stop here every four minutes. After the end of the Second World War, during which the building was badly damaged, and until its final closure in 1952, rail convoys carrying provisions to the surrounding counties departed from this station. In 1961, having fallen into a precarious state of repair, the building was demolished and the ruins restored once more.

But the Kreuzberg district holds several other points of interest for the visitor. Not far from Anhalter Station in Niederkirchner Street, through which the Wall used to pass, as

The remains of Anhalter Station.

can be seen from the ruins which still remain, is the luxurious palace of the **Prussian Parliament (Preußischer Landtag),** where the Berlin parliament has met since 1993, and the **Martin Gropius Bau exhibition centre**. The latter, designed by Martin Gropius, great-uncle of the celebrated Walter Gropius, housed the Berlin Museum of Industrial Art until 1921. After restoration, the building is now used as the venue for important exhibitions. Inside are many beautiful rooms and a courtyard, all decorated with fine plasterwork.

Adjoining Martin Gropius Bau, in Prinz-Albrecht-Gelände, housed in what was the headquarters of the much-feared Gestapo from 1933 to 1945, is the **Topographie des Terror (Topography of Terror)** documentation centre, open to the public. A little further on, in Friedrichstraße, is the well-known frontier post **Checkpoint Charlie**, through which only diplomatic staff and citizens from the Allied nations could pass. Nearby is the **Wall Museum (Mauermuseum)**, containing an exhibition of different devices and inventions used by GDR citizens to attempt to smuggle things from one side of the wall to the other. Finally, the **Berlin Museum (Berlin Museum)** stands in Lindenstraße. This, together with the Märkisches Museum, in Am Köllnischen Park, will soon house the future City of Berlin Museum. The Märkisches Museum will be devoted to the history of the city until 1848, the Berlin Museum from 1848 to the present.

Jewish Museum.

Kreuzberg. View of Berlin Mitte. In front, the new Tempodrome.

The Martin Gropius Bau exhibition centre.

Museum of the Transports.

...and today.

«Checkpoint Charlie», in Friedrichstrasse, at a certain point in time...

The Great Star and the Victory Column.

THE TIERGARTEN, THE CULTURAL FORUM AND POTSDAM SQUARE

The **Tiergarten Park**, which lies in the very heart of the city, is one of the many green spaces in Berlin, and is also one of the best-loved. This 200-hectare park contains many important buildings and even a lake, the Neuer See, where visitors can enjoy a ride on a boat. Originally the Prince Elector's hunting reserve, the park was opened for the enjoyment of the Berlin people in 1717. In the early-19th century, the park was completely reorganised in the style of the English landscape gardens by the royal gardener Peter Joseph Lenné and it has, over the years, been gradually embellished with the addition of new statues and busts. Nonetheless, it was largely destroyed during the war, and most of its trees were cut down to use as fuel in the cold winters of the post-war period. Reconstruction began in 1949 with the planting of new trees. Crossing this great park from east to west is **17 June Street**, in the centre of which, at the point known as the Great Star (Großer Stern), where all the main streets and paths converge according to the plans drawn up by Lenné, stands the **Victory Column (Siegessäule)**. This great sandstone column, 68 metres in height, was built by Heinrich Strack between 1869 and 1873. At the top is the goddess Victory, popularly known to the people of Berlin as «the Golden One», sculpted by Friedrich Drake in remembrance of the many military campaigns successfully undertaken by Prussian armies in the 19th century. The column was orig-

Love-Parade Party.

Views of the Trödelmarkt and...

...the Kunstmarkt in 17 June Street.

Detail of the Victory goddess. At her feet there is a panoramic viewpoint.

inally installed in King's Square, before the Reichstag, and was transferred to preside over the Great Star in 1938-39 as part of the reorganisation of the capital of the Reich. The viewing platform at the feet of the statue, reached by a winding staircase, commands splendid views over the Tiergarten and the entire city.

17 June Street is particularly lively at weekends, as an **art and second hand market (Kunst- und Trödelmarkt)** takes place here every Saturday and Sunday from 8.00 to 17.00. This is the largest flea market in Berlin. Like others, such as the Flohmarkt or the Kunst- und Nostalgiemarkt, both in Mitte district in the eastern part of the city, it is possible to pick up truly original items at this market, as well as relics from the former East Germany.

Adjoining 17 June Street, just before we come to the Brandenburg Gate, is the **Soviet Memorial (Sowjetisches Ehrenmal)**, built in 1945 using ashlar stone from the old Reichskanzlei, soon after the occupation of the city, in honour of the 20,000 Soviet troops who died in the Battle of Berlin.

At the north-west end of the Tiergarten is the **Hansa district (Das Hansaviertel)**, a great urban development dating to 1957 and built on the occasion of the International Architecture Exhibition of that same year. The district is made up of a combination of single-storey houses and blocks of flats, all designed by leading architects such as Walter Gropius and Max Taut, amongst others.

Also the fruit of the 1957 International Architecture Exhibition, or Interbau, is

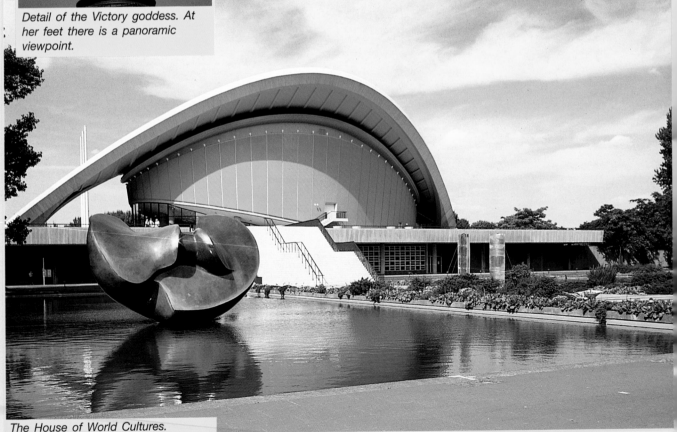

The House of World Cultures.

View of the government's quarter (Regierungviertel). At the background, Berlin Mitte.

The Reichstag.

The Bellevue Palace.

the renowned **Congress Hall (Kongreßhalle)**, the United States' contribution to the event and which has become affectionately known as the «pregnant ostrich» in allusion to the daringly curved shape of its roof and the lake which surrounds the site. The Congress Hall stands in the north-east area of the Tiergarten, near John-Foster-Dulles-Allee Walk. The original roof collapsed in 1980, but the hall was immediately rebuilt and opened again in 1987 to mark the 750th anniversary of the founding of the city. The building now serves as an exhibition centre and as the **House of World Cultures** (Haus der Kulturen der Welt), by which name it has also become known. Besides a large exhibition room, the facilities include a 1,250-seater auditorium used for concerts, film showings and lectures.

Between the World House of Cultures and the Hansa district is Bellevue Palace **(Schloß Bellevue)**. This was built at the command of Prince Ferdinand of Prussia (younger brother of Frederick the Great) between 1785 and 1786 and has been the official residence of the president of the government since 1993.

Opposite Republic Square, at the north-east end of the Tiergarten, is the **Reichstag**. In 1871, after the constitution of the German Reich and the designation of the city of Berlin as the Prussian imperial capital, it was decided to build a new parliamentary seat. To this end, a competition was organised to decide

Berlin Central Station.

The Reichstag.

Details of the Reichstag dome.

who should build it. This having been won by the architect Paul Wallot, Emperor Wilhelm I laid the first stone on 9 June 1884. The work was officially concluded on 5 December 1894 when Emperor Wilhelm II laid the last stone. The dedication «To the German People» over the entrance was added during the First World War. On 9 November 1918, Philipp Scheidemann proclaimed the Republic from one of the windows of the Reichstag. In 1933, the building was partially damaged by a fire, started deliberately, and which became known as the «Reichstag Fire». In 1945, the Soviet flag flew over the sacked ruins of the building. After reunification in December 1990, the first Parliament representing both East and West Germany since the Second World War was convened here, and in 1999, after large-scale reform, the «New Reichstag» was formally inaugurated. The new building is crowned by an impressive 23-metre high glass dome over the chamber, designed, by Sir Norman Foster, and reminiscent of the dome which rose over the original Reichstag.

The Cultural Forum.

In the south-west part of the Tiergarten, near Lützow Square, is the **Bauhaus Archive (Bauhaus-Archiv)**, a building completed in 1978 housing one of the museums conceived by the founder of the Bauhaus movement, Walter Gropius (1883-1969). The museum contains collections of models, drawings, furniture and art and craftwork created at this famed institute of crafts and trades in the period between its establishment in 1919 and its closure in 1933. The centre also organises temporary exhibitions.

Finally, also in the southern sector of the Tiergarten, is the **Cultural Forum (Kulturforum)**, a series of buildings designed in the 1970s with the idea of forming a replica to East Berlin's «museum island». The most important of these buildings are the **Philharmonic**

Room (Philharmonie), with its golden tones, the neighbouring **Musical Instrument Museum (Musikinstrumentenmuseum)**, the **National Library (Staatsbibliothek)** and the **Chamber Music Room (Kamermusiksaal)**. These four buildings were all designed by Hans Scharoun (1893-1972). The first to be completed was the Philharmonic Room in 1963, followed by the Chamber Music Room in 1987, the Musical Instrument Museum in 1984 and, finally, the National Library –also Scharoun's last building– in 1978. The Philharmonic Room, one of the most representative of all the modern buildings in the city and the seat of the Berlin Philharmonic, is famed for its extraordinary acoustics. This is the venue, not only of classical music concerts, but also of the Berlin

Jazz Festival every year from late-October to early-November, whilst the adjoining Chamber Music Room offers the perfect setting for performances by smaller orchestras. For its part, the Musical Instrument Museum contains a collection of over 2,500 instruments. Guided tours of the museum are available and include demonstrations of many of these instruments. Finally, the National Library contains nearly three million volumes.

In this same area, not far from the Cultural Forum, is the **Museum of Applied Art (Kunstgewerbemuseum)**. The museum is housed in a building designed by Rolf Gutbrod and completed between 1973 and 1985. Also nearby are: **Saint Matthew's Church (Matthänskirche)**, built in 1846 by August Stüler; the **Painting**

Museum of Applied Art.

Near the Cultural Forum is the new Regierungsviertel district. In the photo, the new Bundeskanzleramt building.

The New National Gallery, a steel and glass building designed by Mies van der Rohe and completed between 1965 and 1968.

Gallery (Gemäldegalerie), housed in a building inaugurated in 1998 and designed by the architects Heinz Hilmer and Christoph Sattler and containing an exceptional collection of European painting from the 13th century to the present from Dahlem; and Mies van der Rohe's creation in steel and glass which houses the **New National Gallery (Neue Nationalgalerie).** Built between 1965 and 1968, the New National Gallery is the venue for exhibitions of contemporary art.

Behind the Cultural Forum is Potsdam Square. Created during the reign of Friedrich Wilhelm I, this great esplanade was, until the Second World War, the meeting point between east and west Berlin. After the construction of the wall in 1961, however, it became a tragic extension of no-man's-land, and it was not restored to its earlier importance until after German reunification. In 1994, this became the largest area of construction work in Europe, with the participation of such renowned architects as Renzo Piano, Georgio

The Federal Ministry of Defense, in the Stauffenberg street, the 20th of July.

The Potsdam Square in 1980.

Aerial view of the new constructions in Potsdam Square.

Night-time view of Potsdam Square.

The Philharmonic Room and Potsdam Square.

Grassi, Arata Isozaki, Rafael Moneo, Helmut Jahn and Richard Rogers. The results can now be seen. This great new urban complex is made up of hundreds of new homes and offices, as well as the business centres of such prestigious corporations as Daimler Benz and Asean Brown Boveri (ABB), leading hotels, cinemas –including a Cinemax seating 3,500 spectators– a huge casino, the largest in Germany, a monumental music-hall, countless shops, bars and restaurants, and the Sony Center, a complex devoted to the audiovisual world, which also contains media and film libraries.

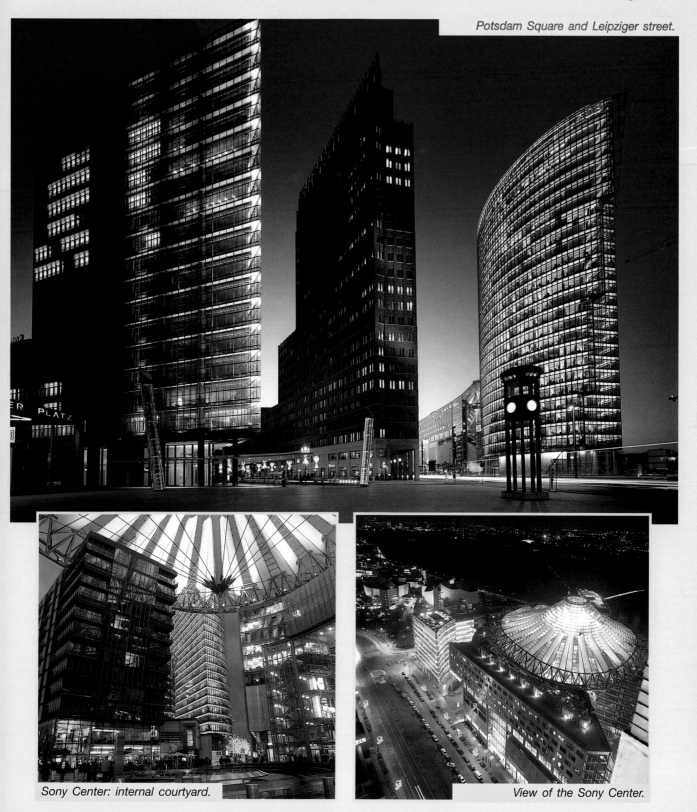

Potsdam Square and Leipziger street.

Sony Center: internal courtyard.

View of the Sony Center.

Zentrum «City West».

KU'DAMM AND ENVIRONS

One of the most frequently photographed places in the city is the point where **Kurfürstendamm** Avenue (popularly known as Ku'damm) meets **Joachimstaler Straße** at Kranzler Corner. On this corner stands, amongst other interesting sights, **Kaiser-Wilhem-Gedächtniskirche (Emperor Wilhelm Commemorative Church),** though everything in Ku'damm makes good photographic material.

The avenue throbs with life, for this is the city's busiest, most varied shopping street, where street sellers, musicians, acrobats and artists of all types vie with one another to catch the attention of passersby or patrons seated at the famous open-air cafés («Strassencafé»). Ku'damm has always been the very personification of the joy of life and originality, an avenue which is at once truly cosmopolitan yet typical of Berlin. Behind the Commemorative Church, in **Breitscheidplatz**, Ku'damm stretches eastwards Wittenbergplatz under the name now of **Tauentzienstraße**. From one end to the other, from Wilmersdorf to Wittenbergplatz, Ku'damm is a total of four kilometres long.

Originally, in the mid-16th century, Ku'damm was a sandy path connecting Berlin with the royal hunting palace of the Prince Electors. This great avenue was given its present appearance in 1880, under Bismarck, and quickly became one of the favourite spots of the people of Berlin, where rich merchants and noblemen and women established their luxurious businesses and residences. Unfortunately, these buildings were devastated during the Second World War.

The imperial period and the modern-day are symbolised simultaneously in a site unique of its type: the **Emperor Wilhelm Commemorative Church**. All that has been conserved of the building, largely destroyed in the war, is the ruined tower, left as a warning. Around this «caried tooth», as it is popularly known, the architect Egon Eiermann built two new buildings between 1961 and 1963, shining blue steel and glass edifices in metallic frames whose interiors are as worthy of interest as are their striking exterior appearance. This mod-

The Commemorative Church and the Europa-Center.

KU'DAMM AND ENVIRONS

Corner of Kranzler with the Victory passage.

Victoria Passage: inside patio.

View of a terrace in Ku'damm.

ern architectural site has become known affectionately to Berliners as «lipstick and powder».

Just opposite the Commemorative Church is **Europa-Center**, a tiny city within a city, with more than one hundred shops and boutiques offering a huge variety of articles, as well as cafeterias, restaurants and cinemas and the famous cabaret Die Stachelschweine («The Porcupines»). Two attractions are particularly worthy of attention: the terrace of the Café Tiffany's and the «Time Flies Clock» (Uhr der fliessenden Zeit), a 13-metre high work by B. Gitton. The Europa-Center was opened in 1965 and soon became a leading attraction for visitors and locals alike. The

Café Tyffany's in the Europa-Center.

Europa-Center: «Time Flies Clock».

Europa-Center: view of the interior.

Zoo: Elephant Gate.

highest building in the complex, crowned by the Mercedes star, 103 metres high, is known as «Little Manhattan».

Between the skyscraper and the Commemorative Church stretches Breitscheidplatz where an original fountain known as the **«Terrestrial Globe»** has stood since 1983. The fountain is 18 metres in diameter, whilst the globe is 4.5 metres high. Nearby is one of the entrances to **Berlin Zoo**. Taken together, Berlin Zoo and Tierpark Berlin-Friedrichsfelde Zoo boast a diversity of species (over 1,500) with few rivals anywhere in the world. The zoo was inaugurated in 1844 after Friedrich Wilhelm IV had donated his private collection to provide the

Aquarium.

Night-time view of Wittenbergplatz and Tauentzienstraße.

The «Terrestrial Globe» fountain in Breitscheidplatz.

oasis. Particularly striking is the Elephant Gate with its oriental-style buildings guarded by two huge stone elephants. Beside the entrance to Berlin Zoo is the **Aquarium**, which houses not only a rich diversity of fresh- and saltwater species, but also a **Terrarium** and the renowned **Insektarium**. All these sections form part of the Zoo, but can be visited separately.

The **sculpture** entitled **«Berlin»**, which stands in Tauentzienstraße, was made by the sculptor Matschinsky-Denninghoff to mark the 750th anniversary of the founding of the city in 1987 for installa-

KU'DAMM AND ENVIRONS

Corner of Ku'damm and Joachimsthaler street with Swisshotel and Wertheim.

The West Theatre and the Stockmarket Building.

tion in the Boulevard of the Sculptures. It symbolises the union and disunion of the then divided city of Berlin. Further on, near Wittenbergplatz metro station, are the famous **Kaufhaus des Westens (Department Stores of the West)** better known by the abbreviated name of Ka De We. Founded in around 1900, this store forms an integral part of the history of the city and is now one of the largest and most modern shopping centres on the entire continent. The seven floors of this great emporium display all kinds of goods, something to satisfy any desire, whether large or small, no matter how extravagant or exotic, indeed the management takes particular pride in this. On the sixth floor is the universally famous «gourmet's paradise». Here, for example, customers can choose from amongst over 1,800 different types of cheese.

Another large shopping centre of long tradition in the city of Berlin is **Wertheim**, located in Ku'damm near the Commemorative Church. Wertheim's windows attractive glass front, several stories high, are always originally and strikingly decorated. Nonetheless, the principal attraction here is under the roof of the building: a panoramic restaurant arranged in different squares, avenues and cafés between fountains and pools, commanding magnificent views over West Berlin.

Before leaving this area, we should not fail to mention several other points of interest, such as the **Theater des Westens (West Theatre)**, at number 12 Kantstraße Berlin's most renowned music and operetta theatre, housed in a building in the Belle Epoque style and dating from 1896, and, most especially, the cafés and restaurants which line Ku'damm and adjacent streets.

THE HOUSE OF THE JEWISH COMMUNITY AND THE NEW SYNAGOGUE

The new **Jüdisches Gemeindehaus (House of the Jewish Community)** was built between 1957 and 1959 in Fasanenstraße, a street running perpendicular to Ku'damm. This was also the site of the original synagogue, built by Ehrenfried between 1910 and 1912 in a Romanesque-Byzantine style. Of that impressive original building which, like many others, was destroyed on Cristalsnacht («The Night of the Broken Glass»), 9 November 1938, all that remains to remind us is the portal of the original entrance, which was incorporated into the new construction. The black sculpture in the square opposite the building represents the destruction of a Tora.

Also set fire to on that lamentable night in 1938 was the synagogue situated at number 30 Oranienburger Straße, north of the historic city which, since its construction in 1866, had been the centre of the social and spiritual life of the Jewish community in Berlin. Later, in 1943, the building itself was devastated during the bombing of the city. The **Neue Synagoge (New Synagogue)** began to be built in 1988. Its most striking element is the oriental-style domes which crown it. The main room in the church can be observed from the «Centrum Judaicum», a museum first opened in 1995 and which illustrates the history of vicissitudes suffered by the synagogue, and the history of the Berlin Jews.

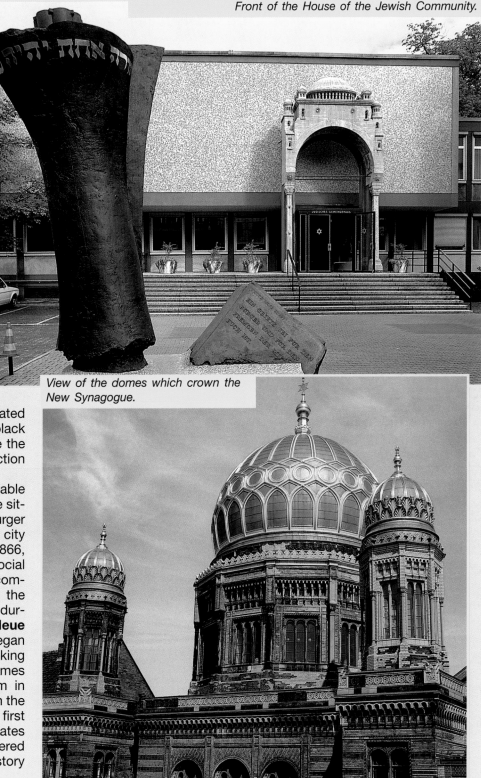

Front of the House of the Jewish Community.

View of the domes which crown the New Synagogue.

The Memorial to the murdered Jews of Europe, by Peter Eisenman.

Zoo Station.

CHARLOTTENBURG

17 June Street stretches westwards to the Charlottenburg district, terminating in Ernst-Reuter Square, presided over by the buildings of the **Technical University (Technische Universität)**, before continuing under the name, firstly, of Bismarck and then of Kaiserdamm. This first stretch, Bismarckstraße, contains two leading cultural centres: the Schiller Theatre, at number 110, and the Berlin German Opera at number 35. The **Schiller Theatre (Schiller-Theater)** was built between 1905 and 1906, but was badly damaged during the Second World War. The new theatre was opened in 1951 and went on to become one of the finest venues for classical theatre in

the German tongue, though since its recent privatisation the main fare on the theatre programme has been musicals imported from New York. The **Berlin German Opera (Deutsche Oper Berlin)** is another modern edifice, built in reinforced concrete and glass between 1956 and 1961 according to plans drawn up by Ernst Bornemann. The productions staged here, particularly as regards ballet, are renowned the world over, and the casts of operas produced here inevitably include many of the great international names of *il bel canto*.

At the end of Kaiserdamm, near Masurenalle Avenue, is the trade fair, formed by a number of pavilions, the **ICC (International Congress Centre)** and one of the most popular of

Berlin's identifying symbols: the **Communications Tower (Funkturm)**. The ICC, a building like an interplanetary spaceship from a science fiction coming down to land, was built between 1975 and 1979 to replace the old Tiergarten congress hall, no longer large enough to meet modern requirements. The new complex is truly monstrous in size: 320 metres long by 80 metres wide and 40 metres high, with 8 halls and 70 conference rooms with total capacity of 20,300.

Opposite the ICC stands «Lanky», as the Berliners know the Communications Tower. Opened in 1926 on the occasion of the Third Radio-transmission Exhibition, the tower was fortunate enough to survive the

The ICC and the Communications Tower.

war unscathed. Some 135 metres high (150 if we include the aerial), a platform 55 metres above the ground contains a restaurant offering panoramic views of the city, whilst the tower also contains another viewing point 125 metres above ground level. Not far from this point, on the other side of Masurenalle Avenue towards Theodor-Heuss Square, is the **SFB (Sendes Freies Berlin-Radio Free Berlin)** broadcasting centre, with its television and radio studios, built between 1963 and 1971 by the architects Robert Tepez and Annelies Zander.

Further west of Charlottenburg, near Reichsstraße, is the **Olympic Stadium (Olympiastadion)**. Built on the site of the old Reich Stadium for the 1936 Olympic Games by the architects Werner and Walter March, and refurbished in 2004 to host the 2006 Football World Cup. Even today, this monumental construction causes a powerful impression, for it is a huge cement oval measuring some 300 metres in length by 230 metres in width and an exemplary model of architectural achievement. The stadium, which witnessed the triumph of

many great athletes, striving to win the gold medal, such as Jesse Owens, holds around 90,000 spectators.

Behind the Olympic Ring, going west, on a small hill, is the **Waldbühne («theatre in the wood»)**. This is an open-air venue built like a classical amphitheatre and which holds 20,000 spectators. Over the last few years, this has become one of the favourite summertime meeting-places amongst the people of Berlin. Here, under the ghostly light of candles or under the hot summer sun, over a glass of wine, a soft drink or a sandwich, those assembled enjoy the melodies of classical or pop music concerts of the highest order. This «green arena» is also popular for its open-air film sessions. Nonetheless, this is also a place of unhappy memories as in 1967, during a concert at the Waldbühne given by the Rolling Stones, the facilities were entirely destroyed.

This stroll around Charlottenburg ends in Spandau Avenue, where we find the main entrance to **Charlottenburg Castle**. Since the destruction of the City Castle (Stadtschloßes) in 1950, Charlottenburg is the only building dating back to the times of the Hohenzollerns still standing in Berlin. Friedrich III commissioned the Master Nering to build the castle in 1695 as a summer residence for his wife,

«Waldwühne».

The Olympic Stadium.

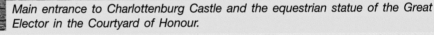

Main entrance to Charlottenburg Castle and the equestrian statue of the Great Elector in the Courtyard of Honour.

Princess Sophie Charlotte. Rather small for the taste of the day (only the central body was originally built), the castle stood facing the entry gate to Old Berlin, near the village of Lietzow. The castle was extended for the first time to mark the coronation of the Elector as King of Prussia (1701), and was constantly modified and extended over the course of the next one hundred years. On the death of Sophie Charlotte, the edifice, originally known as Lietzenburg, was renamed Charlottenburg Castle.

In front of the central body, surrounded by wrought-iron railings, is the Square of Honour, presided over by the equestrian statue of the Elector, whose son, King Friedrich I, commissioned Andreas Schlüter to execute it in memory of his father in 1696. This majestic sculpture was originally installed on the Long Bridge (Langen Brücke), now Rathausbrücke or Town Hall Bridge, in the city centre, and was brought to Charlottenburg in 1952. Some of the castle rooms are open to the public, including the sumptuous chambers of Frederick the Great. The magnificent site is completed by the **Castle Park (Schloßgarten)**, the oldest of the gardens conserved in Berlin. The park, arranged in the style of the French baroque gardens, was transformed into an English landscape garden in the late-18th century by

Lenné. The most interesting features of the park include the **Belvedere Tea House**, built in 1788 at the command of Friedrich II and containing magnificent collections from the old Royal Porcelain Factory of Prussia (KPM, Königlich Preußischen Porzellanmanufaktur); the **Mausoleum,** built between 1810 and 1812 by Friedrich III to house his own mortal remains and those of his wife, Queen Louise, who died very young; and the **Schinkel Pavilion**, a tiny, exquisite summer house which Friedrich III commissioned Schinkel to build in 1824 for himself and his second wife, Princess Liegnitz.

Also of outstanding interest is the **Knobelsdorff Wing** of the castle, thus known in honour of the architect who built it. This wing houses a collection of Romantic painting, including such masterpieces as Spitzweg's «The Old Poet», as well as works by masters from Watteau to Caspar David Friedrich. On the opposite side of the avenue, facing the castle, are three interesting museums: the **Egyptian Museum**, with pieces including the famed bust of Nefertiti; the **Berggruen Collection**, with a large number of paintings, sculptures and sketches by eight great artists (Picasso, Klee, Cézanne, Matisse, van Gogh, Braque, Laurens and Giacometti), brought together by art collector Heinz Berggruen and donated to the city; and the **Brohän Museum**, which houses the collection of Hamburg businessman Karl Bröhan, also donated to the city, and which includes furniture, paintings and industrial design objects from the period from the Paris Universal Exhibition of 1889 and the beginning of the Second World War.

Charlottenburg and the castle gardens.

Tropical greenhouse in the Botanical Gardens.

THE BOTANICAL GARDENS AND THE MUSEUMS OF DAHLEM

The idea of creating a new **Botanical Garden (Botanischer Garten)** between Lichterfelde and Dahlem arose towards the end of the 19th century, when the capacity of the old Schöneberg gardens had become exhausted. The new gardens were built under the direction of the botanist Adolf Engler and were opened in 1910. This great garden, occupying a 42-hectare site, contains a varied wealth of flora made up of some 18,000 species, making it one of the most impressive collections of its kind in the world. In the centre rises the surprising form of the Tropical Greenhouse, an architectural marvel whose interior houses veritable tropical landscapes. Also interesting is the «Victoria Amazonica» greenhouse, which contains giant amphibious plants of that same name, as well as the new Cactus Greenhouses. The entrances to the Botanical Garden are in Königin-Luise Street and Unter den Eichen Avenue. The visit is highly recommended, both to plant-lovers and those looking for an enjoyable stroll.

Not far from the Botanical Garden, between Arnimallee and Lansstraße, is the Dahlem complex, built in 1921 at the initiative of Wilhelm von Bode. Here we find four interesting museums, brought together in one building: the **Indian Art Museum,** the **Museum of Islamic Art**, the **Museum of Far Eastern Art** and the **Ethnological Museum**. This last is perhaps the most attractive to visitors, as it brings together exceptional works from all the corners of the earth, as well as many unusual pieces collected by the Elector in the 17th century.

Partial aerial view of Spandau and Scharfen Lanke Bay.

BERLIN, BETWEEN THE SPREE AND THE HAVEL

To the west, the district of Charlottenburg ends at the River Havel, which winds its way through a 30 kilometres of the city. Just as the Spree in the south-east flows into Lake Müggelsee, the waters of the Havel in the south-west go to form Lake Wannsee (Großer Wannsee), with its many bays, beaches and jetties, and where boats from the so-called «White Fleet» offer trips to such places as the Wannsee neighbour-hood, the city centre or the Köpenick district.

Spandau, which lies at the meeting point of the Havel and the Spree, is an ancient settlement that was granted its charter in 1232 and was absorbed by the city of Berlin in 1920. The most interesting feature here is the Altstadt area, or old city, with its houses and the Church of Saint Nicholas, built in the 15th century, though baroque and Gothic Revival elements were added subsequently, and the Citadel (Zitadelle), a 16th century fortress built on the site of a castle going back to the

12th century. It was in the Julius Tower, part of the original Spandau Castle, that the «Reich War Treasures» were kept from 1874 to 1919.

Grunewald Wood stretches out between Spandau and Lake Wannsee, occupying an area of over 30 km^2. Here we find the Grunewald Tower, a 50-metre-high construction built in 1897 by Franz Heinrich Schwechten.

Below, **Swan Island (Schwanenwerder)** and, beyond, the **Great Wannsee (Großer Wannsee)** lake with the beach of the same name (Strandbad Wannsee), opened in 1907. A popu-

BERLIN, BETWEEN THE SPREE AND THE HAVEL

The River Spree with the Molecule Man sculpture.

Köpenick pier.

Köpenick Palace.

Main gate to the Spandau citadel and the Julius Tower.

The Grunewald Tower from the Havel.

The «Federal Press Beach».

Wannsee beach.

Pfaueninsel Castle (Peacock Island).

lar leisure site amongst Berliners, 80 metres wide and 1,300 metres long, this is considered to be Europe's largest inland beach.

To the west, following the course of the Havel, we soon reach **Peacock Island (Pfaueninsel)**, a 76-hectare islet which can be reached only by a ferry and that only at limited times. A visit to this island is one of the outstanding features in a visit to Berlin due to its wealth of flora and birdlife and its beautiful castle, built as if in ruins. This castle was designed by Brendl between 1794 and 1797, commissioned by Friedrich Wilhelm II, grandson and successor to Frederick the Great, and his wife. The exquisite nature reserve on the island, however, was marked out later, in 1822, by the then most prestigious landscape gardener in Prussia, Peter Joseph Lenné, who also designed the Tiergarten park and the gardens of Charlottenburg Castle. Finally, farther south or at the end of Königstraße as we look towards Potsdam, is the **Glienicker Bridge (Glienicker Brücke)**. Some 300 metres in length, built originally of wood during the reign of Friedrich Guillermo, Glienicker Bridge, with the vicissitudes of the Second World War at an end and the Wall demolished, has now been restored as the quickest and easiest route between Berlin and the neo-classical **Glienicke Palace (Schloß Glienicke)** and Potsdam. Destroyed by German soldiers in 1945, the bridge was rebuilt in 1950, its centre serving as the frontier between East and West during the period of the isolation of Berlin. Throughout this period, the bridge could only be crossed by members of the Allied military mission and accredited diplomats. It was during these times that Glienicker Bridge became famed as the scene of dramatic exchanges of spies.

Glienicker bridge.

BERLIN'S AIRPORTS

The monument to the Berlin Airlift at Tempelhof Airport, popularly known as the «Hungerkralle» («Rake of Hunger»).

South of Kreuzberg is **Tempelhof Airport**, which first opened in 1923 and handled all civil and military air traffic in West Berlin until 1974, when Tegel Airport entered into service. Standing before Tempelhof Airport entrance hall, in Airlift Square, is a sculpture made in 1951 according to a design by Edward Ludwig to commemorate the blockade Berlin suffered from 23 June 1948 to 12 May 1949, when the Soviets cut off all communications by land and sea with the western part of the city and surrounding area. The famous monument, which symbolises the three air corridors to West Germany, is known to the people of Berlin as the «Rake of Hunger», for those three corridors were used by the legendary aircraft known as «Raisin Bombers» to supply West Berlin throughout the blockade.

As we have mentioned, **Tegel Airport** entered into service in 1974 as the successor to Tempelhof as Berlin's main airport, though its aviation history goes back much further. It was in the airborne battalion's manoeuvre ground here, for

Tegel Airport.

example, that Count Zeppelin landed his LZ3 in 1909. Later, in the 1930s, this was the scene of missile launch tests carried out by Rudolf Nebel, Hermann Oberth and Wernher von Braun. Due to rapidly increasing air traffic, the airport was reorganised, its capacity extended to up to ten million passengers per year. Now that Berlin has been restored as the German capital, moreover, plans have been drawn up not only to remodel **Schönefeld Airport** in South Berlin, but also to build a great airport outside the metropolitan area.

Partial view of Tegel Airport.

FLUGHAFEN BERLIN-SCHÖNEFELD

Schönefeld Airport.

POTSDAM

Sans-Souci Palace.

POTSDAM

Potsdam, a visit not to be missed, lies just outside the gates of Berlin. The air of this former residential city of the princes of Brandenburg and, since 1701, of the Prussian kings, is steeped in the spirit of the Hohenzollerns. In 1945, it was the scene of Allied negotiations over the future of Germany (the Treaty of Potsdam, signed in the Cecilianhof Palace), and the former municipal capital is the capital of the Land of Brandenburg. Potsdam's finest jewel is the **Sans-Souci Palace (Schloß Sans-Souci)** and gardens, occupying a 290-hectare site. King Friedrich Wilhelm I ordered the construction here of the Slav

colony, mentioned earlier, in the year 993, and the Prince Elector Friedrich Wilhelm built a palace on the site in 1600. The real Potsdam, that is to say, the baroque residential city, grew up between 1715 and 1720 when Friedrich Wilhelm I decreed the construction of barracks to house his guard of «tall boys» (grenadiers) in the new township. In 1745, Friedrich II commissioned his master of works, Hans Geog von Knobelsdorff, with the construction of a small palace of truly modest proportions on a terraced site occupied by vineyards. This was where Friedrich wished to spend his leisure hours, in peace, free of the heavy everyday load and far from worldly worries –Sans-Souci («with-

out problems» in French). A statesman, flautist, philosopher and poet the king himself drew up the sketches for this new palace of his, «which knew nothing of worries».
From the same period as the Sans Souci palace are: the **Chinese House (Chinesisches Haus)**, built by J. G Büring between 1754 and 1757 **Neptune's Grotto**, the work o Knobelsdorff and completed between 1751 and 1757; the **Painting Galler (Bildergalerie)**, one of the oldest mu seums in Germany, whose construc tion dates to 1755-1764; and the **New Chambers (Neuen Kammern)**, buil in 1747 and converted into a resi dence by the master Knobelsdorff be tween 1771 and 1775.

Sans-Souci Palace: Library.

Marble Room.

Small Gallery.

Partial view of one of the bedrooms.

Sans-Souci Palace: the old mill.

Portrait of Frederick the Great.

Concert room, Supra Park.

Guest bedroom.

Open cupboard in the Library.

Guest bedroom.

Chinese House.

The dome.

Mural paintings.

Cornet music.

Eating melons.

Violinist.

The Painting Gallery.

The Painting Gallery: artistic chimney.

At the end of the Seven Years' War (1756-1763), Prussian power and glory were exalted in an imposing monument, the **New Palace (Neues Palais)**, built between 1763 and 1769 by J. G. Büring and H. C. Manger. This palace, 240 long with 200 richly-decorated rooms, is adorned by 292 sandstone sculptures, 196 angels and stone laurel wreaths, and is crowned by an enormous dome. Behind the New Palace stand the **Commons (Communs)**, built 1766-1769 for different uses and to house the palace servants and retinue.

Sans-Souci Park underwent a second phase of construction under Friedrich Wilhelm IV, who came to the throne in 1840. Whilst crown

The Communities' Building.

Aerial view of the New Palace with the Communities' Building.

Palace theatre.

Breakfast room, in the upper area.

Marble Room.

Women's Bedroom, in the lower area.

Marble Gallery.

Grotto Room.

The New Palace.

Charlottenhof Castle.

Charlottenhof: dining-room.

The Krongut Bornstedt royal estate.

The Roman Baths: the Caldarium.

The Impluvium.

Two views of the Atrium.

Orangery.

Orangery: Raphael Room.

prince, Friedrich Wilhelm ordered the construction of **Charlottenhof Castle (Schloß Charlottenhof)**, built by Schinkel in an austere neo-classical style between 1826 and 1829, the **Roman Baths (Römische Bäder)** and the **Court Gardener's House** in 1829 and the **Orangery (Orangerie)**, designed in 1828 and built between 1851 and 1860. The Orangery, whose front is 300 metres in length, contains many sumptuously-decorated rooms.

The city of Potsdam itself also contains many other interesting buildings. In Luisenplatz, beside Sans-Souci Park, is the **Brandenburg Gate (Brandenburger Tor)**, a triumphal arch built in 1771 by K. v. Goutard and G. C. Unger to commemorate the Seven Years' War. From here, the pedestrian street leads to Bassinplatz. Not far off to the south lies the **Old Market (Altes Markt)**, with the **Church of Saint Nicholas (Nikolaikirche)**, built according to plans drawn up by Schinkel between 1830 and 1837, and the **Old Town Hall (Altes Rathaus)**, built in 1753 by J. Boumann. Between Bassinplatz and the **New Gate (Nauener Tor)**, a Gothic Revival work dating to 1755, lies the **Dutch Quarter (Hölland Viertel)** a residential district of traditional Dutch-style houses built between 1734 and 1742 by craftsmen brought here from Holland by Frederick the Great to work on Sans-Souci Park.

Further north, on the banks of Lake Heiligen, stands the **Marble Palace (Marmorpalais)**, a brick and Silesian marble construction which was

Dragon House (Drachenhaus) and Marble Palace.

Cecilienhof Castle.

Cecilienhof Castle.

the favourite residence of Friedrich Wilhelm II.

Also in the north of Potsdam is the **Russian Colony (Russische Kolonie)**, an area of Russian-style houses built in 1826 by order of Friedrich II (the most outstanding features of this zone are the Russian Orthodox church, built in 1829) and **Cecilienhof Castle (Schloß Cecilienhof)**. The latter is particularly famed as the venue of the Potsdam Conference in the summer of 1945, where the heads of state of the victorious allies, Stalin, Truman and Attlee (who had replaced Churchill), decided the fate of post-war Germany. Many of the castle's rooms are open to the public, including that containing the round table where the Potsdam Agreement was signed. Cecilienhof was built between 1913 and 1916 as the residence of the son of Kaiser Wilhelm II and his wife, Cecilia. It was designed by P. S. Naumburg, who took the English country house as his inspiration. Besides the historic apartments, the castle also houses an hotel and a restaurant.

Crown prince's office
(Soviets' office).

Princess's room (North Americans' office).

Crown prince's dressing-room.

Conference room vestibule.

Crown prince's library (British room).

Aerial view of Potsdam, the Havel and Grunewald; in the background we can make out the city of Berlin. In the foreground, Old Market Square with the Church of St. Nicholas and the Old Town Hall.

Potsdam: Gothic Library.

Sanssouci-Belvedere park.

A house of the Russian Colony.

The old mill.

Russian Church of St. Alexander Niewski.

The Peace Church (Friedenskirche).

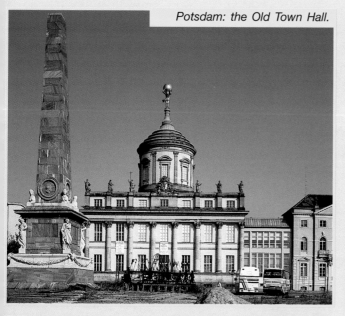

Potsdam: the Old Town Hall.

The Dutch district.

The Filmmuseum (Breite Straße).

Brandenburger street.

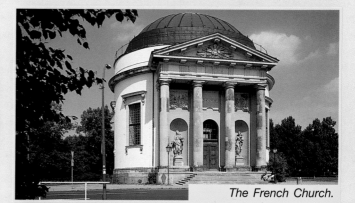

The French Church.

Hunter's Gate.

Nauen Gate.

The Military Orphanage (Breite Straße).

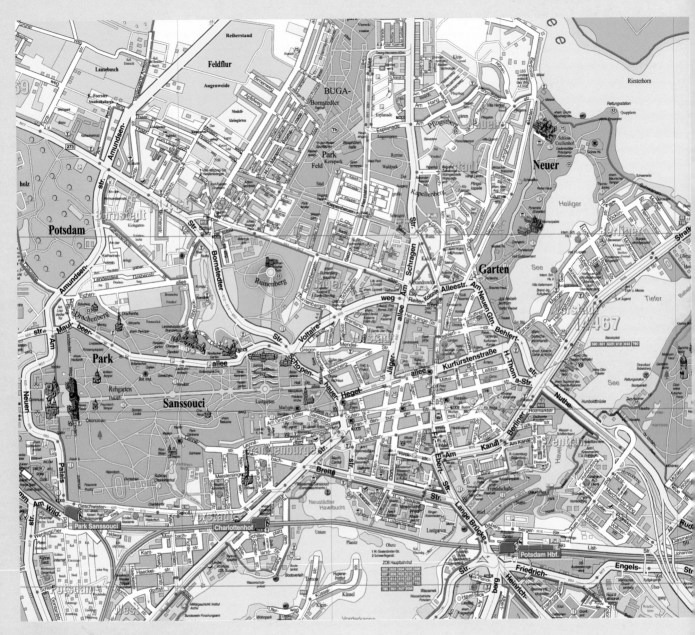

EDITORIAL FISA ESCUDO DE ORO, S.A.
Veneçuela, 105 - 08019 Barcelona
Tel: 93 230 86 00 - www.eoro.com

I.S.B.N. 978-84-378-1532-9
Printed in Spain
Legal Dep. B. 879-2007

Protegemos el bosque; papel procedente de cultivos forestales controlados
Wir schützen den Wald. Papier aus kontrollierten Forsten.
We protect our forests. The paper used comes from controlled forestry plantations
Nous sauvegardons la forêt: papier provenant de cultures forestières contrôlées